FOOD
FACES

FOOD FACES

150 Feasts for the Eyes

RUDI SODAMIN

CULINARY POP ARTIST

FOREWORD BY
THOMAS KELLER

WELCOME BOOKS
A Division of Rizzoli New York

CONTENTS

ARTIST'S STATEMENT

I began to create and photograph stylized food faces as a way to inspire and transform people's relationship with the culinary elements I know so well. I chose to use a whimsical approach as a way to inspire and share positive, universal emotions. My reward is seeing the irrepressible smiles that my works bring to all who see them, and the sense I get of having been able to make a difference in people's lives.

Working like a contemporary Arcimboldo, I intend my stylized food faces to summon visceral and organic sensibilities that reflect the gastronomic diversity of human experience. Through simple portraits created from ingredients found around the globe, I emphasize the universality of both food and art. All humans, regardless of race, gender, experience, or social status, can communicate and connect through food.

FOREWORD

Aside from its obvious utilitarian function, food can be a lot of fun. That's clear from the work of some of our most imaginative chefs. And it's evident in the whimsical creations of my friend, Master Chef Rudi Sodamin, the culinary pop artist behind this delightful book.

Rudi has a keen eye, a wonderfully playful sensibility, and a willingness to let inspiration take him where it will. His face plates were born of humble beginnings. Rudi was just "noodling around the kitchen," looking for ways to make himself and his family smile, when the idea struck him. From that first installation, an art form arose—one that leaves me smiling, too.

Like an inventive chef, Rudi approaches food with a fresh perspective. Over the course of my career, I've prepared beets in more ways than I can count. But I never dreamed of "The Beet Creature" marrying beets with rosemary and morel mushrooms to create a most curious countenance. The first time I laid eyes on this composition, I laughed out loud at its zaniness and charm. "Tiny Zucchini" had a similar effect on me, as did "Cranky Risotto," whose grouchy expression still makes me grin from ear to ear. And then there's my personal favorite, "Monsieur Aubergine." Don't let his sophisticated Francophone name fool you: he's as endearingly goofy as any vegetable-based character you'll ever meet.

Grainy Grins, Fruity Actors, Veggie Whimsy. I could go on. But better to let you flip through these pages to discover its pleasures and surprises for yourself.

Food is nourishment, of course. But it also helps sustain us through the happy memories it makes. Through his food faces, Rudi puts happiness front and center. On a plate. Go ahead and find the faces that inspire you!

THOMAS KELLER, Chef/Proprietor The French Laundry

FACE TO FACE
MY CREATIVE VISION

Since I first stood at my mother's side in our kitchen in Austria when I was twelve years old, I thought of food as paint. It is the paint of our lives. Its colors both stimulate and nourish us. At a young age, I was taken with the idea that the way you present the food to the people who eat it helps them understand that each meal is a beautiful gift.

To me, food is love, expression, emotion, and art. It transcends language, speaking to us through aroma, texture, smell, taste, and memory. It captures both the eye and the imagination through a vibrant colorful interplay.

I was immensely lucky to have been born with an appreciation of and instinct toward creativity. I have cultivated my creative sense through my chosen profession as a Chef—since the very beginning, I have been known for my imaginative culinary presentations. My passion for food, people, and forward-driving culinary, cultural, and business vision is driven by this same restless creative exploration and discovery.

It always starts the same way—with a creative exploration. For example, a few years ago, I was noodling around in my kitchen, feeling particularly inspired and whimsical, and I made a simple happy face on my plate with some simple ingredients. It made me smile. I began making face plates with meals for my partner, my kids, my friends, and, each time, the response was always the same—a big, honest smile of delight and surprise, and a single word: "Wow!"

The results positively delighted me. There was something so compelling to me about these photographs, and I enjoyed the process so much, that I created another, and another. Over time, I had created hundreds, and gave birth to an obsession. My hobby become an artistic passion. This unique artwork started with a simple creative food face idea and is now being printed on fine china.

Whenever I saw food ingredients at the market, whenever I got the chance, I would bring one of my sketches to life on a plate or canvas, shopping for just the right ingredients and excited to see each personality emerging as I placed the ingredients.

My photo shoots became more and more elaborate, incorporating greater technology and lighting techniques as I began diligently capturing my gallery-worthy photography of these delicious characters. The process both entertained and captivated me. At first, I thought this was just an interesting idea to pursue for my own satisfaction, but the more images I produced, the more I understood that this effort was far more than a pastime—I was creating a serious body of work through an artistic process that had never been done before by any artist or professional chef.

I began slowly to show my growing collection to international artists, culinary colleagues, and friends around the globe. One curator boldly proclaimed that I was the Arcimboldo of the modern age. I don't know about that, but I've created this book because, aside from my pleasure in the process, there has been one constant—I have never shown anyone either a single picture or a group of my food faces, that a smile did not widen across the viewer's own.

As an artist and a chef, it would be hard to enjoy any higher praise.

RUDI SODAMIN

FRUIT
ACTORS

AUNT ZESTY

MON CHERIE

18

MANGO TANGO

BERRY AWAKENING

HAWAIIAN SUNSHINE

KUMQUAT'S UP

NAPA TWILIGHT

Food, like a loving touch

or a glimpse of divine power,

has that ability to comfort

NORMAN KOLPAS

MIAMI LIMEY

HOT DATE

MAMMA MIA

CURRENT TEEN

SHY GUY

SUMMER BABE

MAD SCIENTIST

First we eat, then

we do everything else.

M. F. K. FISHER

ARCIMBOLDO HOMAGE

THE PROFESSOR

MADAME STRAWBERRY

RASPUTIN

SUSPICIOUS DETECTIVE

BOO MCFIG

TOMATO KISS

LOLITA

CHEER ME UP!

VEGGIE
WHIMSY

BURNING PASSION

MONA PUMPKIN

46

MINNIE ASPARAGOOSE

INSPECTOR BUTTERNUT

48

HONEY PUMPKIN

MRS. VEGGIE

50

NEW DELHI DELISH

BACKYARD BOB

ROSALINDA CHOY

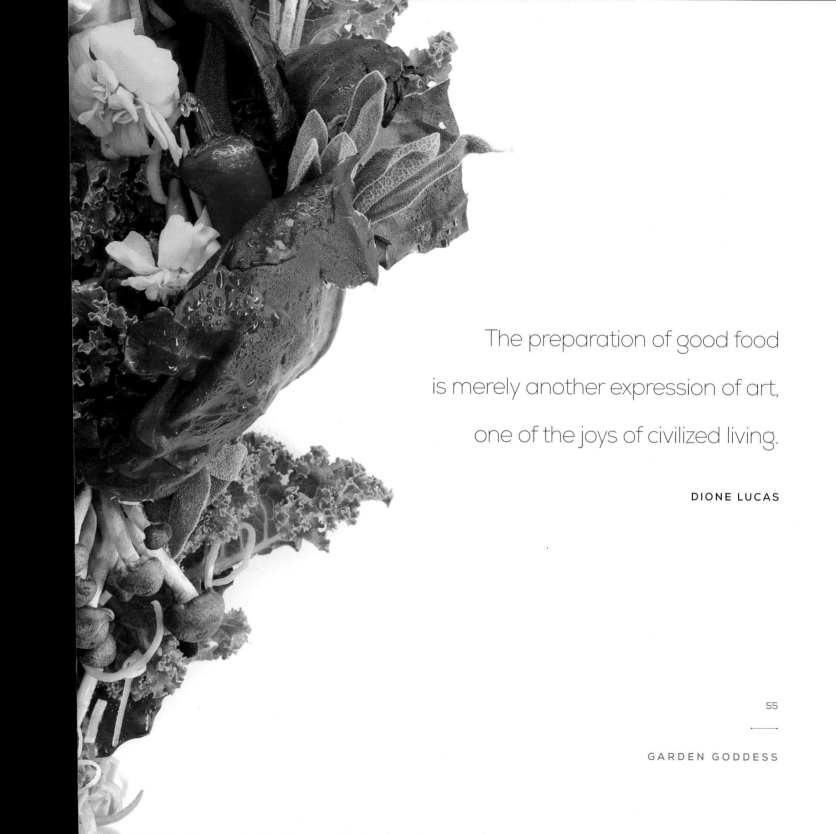

The preparation of good food

is merely another expression of art,

one of the joys of civilized living.

DIONE LUCAS

RUFFLES LACY

CARROT GLORY

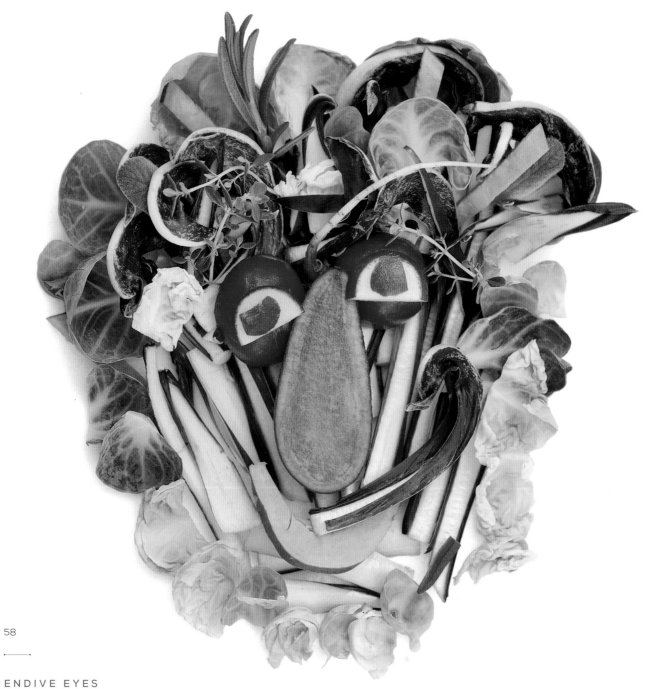

ENDIVE EYES

SPINACH FAIR

MAD BEETS

AH MAIZE

LIFE GURU

SISTER MELANGE

BEET CREATURE

TINY ZUCCHINI

BRAINY CELERIAC

A DAY IN BRUSSELS

68

MAMMA MINESTRONE

Cookery is not chemistry.
It is an art. It requires
instinct and taste rather than
exact measurements.

MARCEL BOULESTIN

71

JOLLY CAULI

HYPNOTIC GAL

SPIKY ADAM

WEIRDO

HOLY GUACAMOLE

CHICKEN SOUPY SOUL

PARSNIP SCHNOZZOLA

NOSE RING ALIEN

POTATO PETE

BLOOMIE LOCKS

GOBBLE VEGGIES

82

DRESSED FOR SUCCESS

83

CABBAGE PATCH KID

GREEN GAZE

HOT CINNAMON EXTRA VIRGIN

CRY BABY

Cooking is like love.

It should be entered into with

abandon or not at all.

HARRIET VAN HORNE

TRY ME; I'M HOT!

LEEK TRESSES

MONSIEUR AUBERGINE

DAHL TURBAN

DILLY FRUITY

BANGLADISH

HI, STRANGER

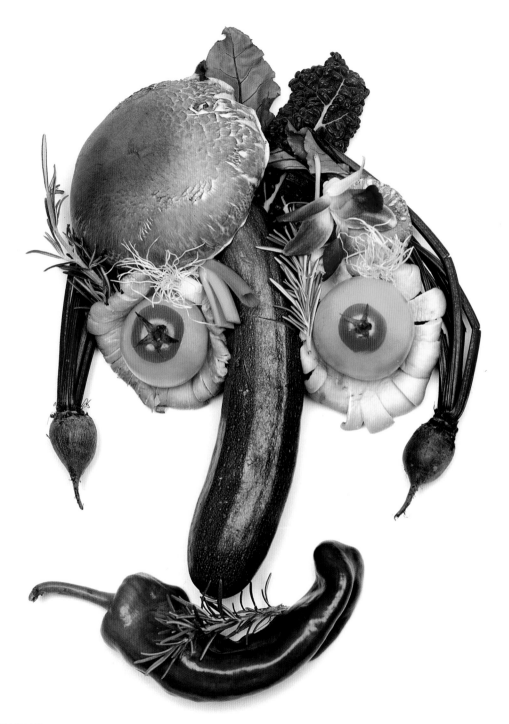

MAKE ME CURIOUS

HAVE A GOOD DAY, HONEY

HAPPY WEDDING

HANGOVER CURE

GARDEN DIET

HAIRY DAYS

MEAT & FISH FACADES

THE CLAWED CADET

SMOKED ROE BEARD

FILET JONNIE

MY AUSTRIAN BREAKFAST

DON'T LOOK SO CRABBY

FIERY UPDO

MOLTO TOTTO

SURFY TURFY

Laughter is brightest

where food is best.

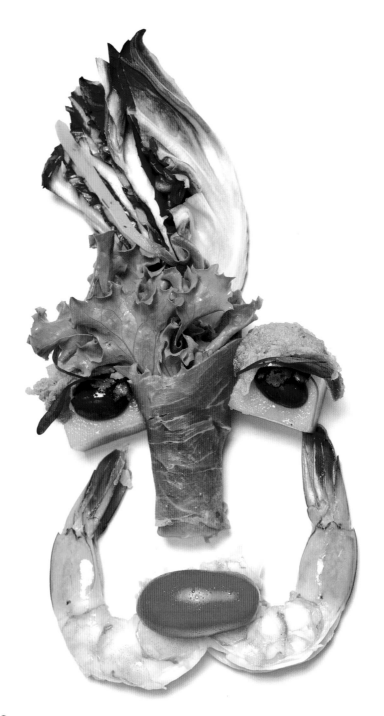

YOU TALKIN' TO ME?

SUSHI GALORE

MAKE SOMEONE HAPPY

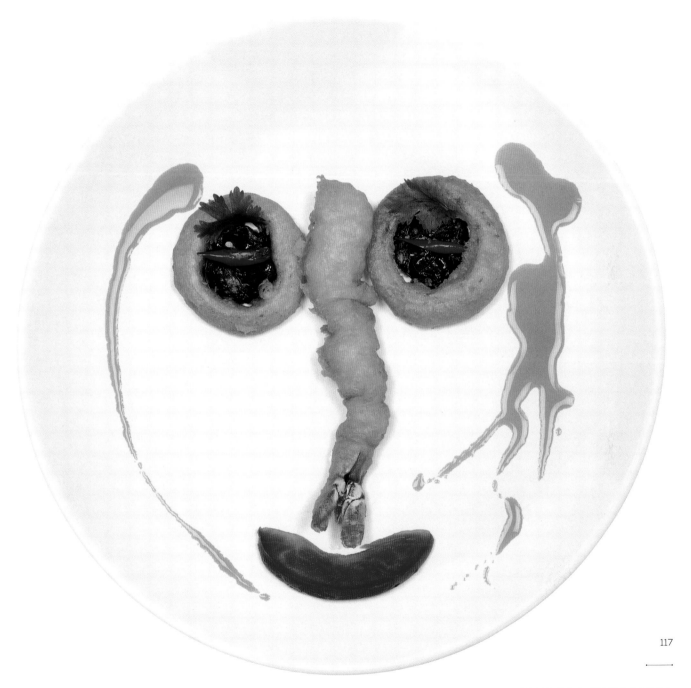

TEMPURA TEMPTRESS

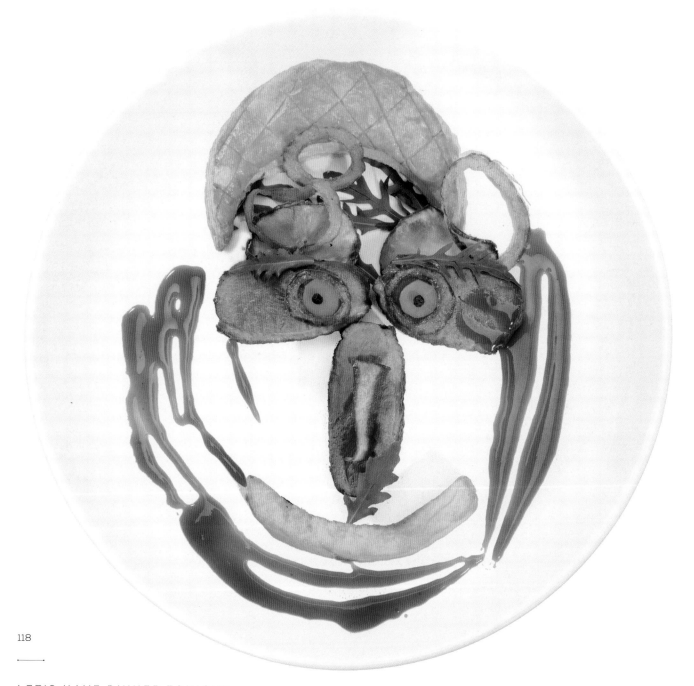

LET'S HAVE DINNER TONIGHT

SHELLY

KING SALMON

MADEMOISELLE ESCARGOT

The gentle art of gastronomy

is a friendly one. It hurdles

the language barrier, makes

friends among civilized people,

and warms the heart.

SAMUEL CHAMBERLAIN

MON MOULES SEL DE MER

MADAME LOBSTER

PEA PUP

SEAWEEDO

SALMON CAVIAR QUEEN

SASSY SUSHI

CATCH ME IF YOU CAN

CLOWN

NONO VERMICELLI IN HIS SUSHI CAPPELLO

FISHERMAN JON

133

There is no sincerer love

than the love of food.

GEORGE BERNARD SHAW

FISH DUDE

BISQUE-Y BUSINESS

MONEY HONEY

LOVE MY 'DO

NORWEGIAN BEAUTY

WHAT A CATCH!

KOOKY SPOOKY

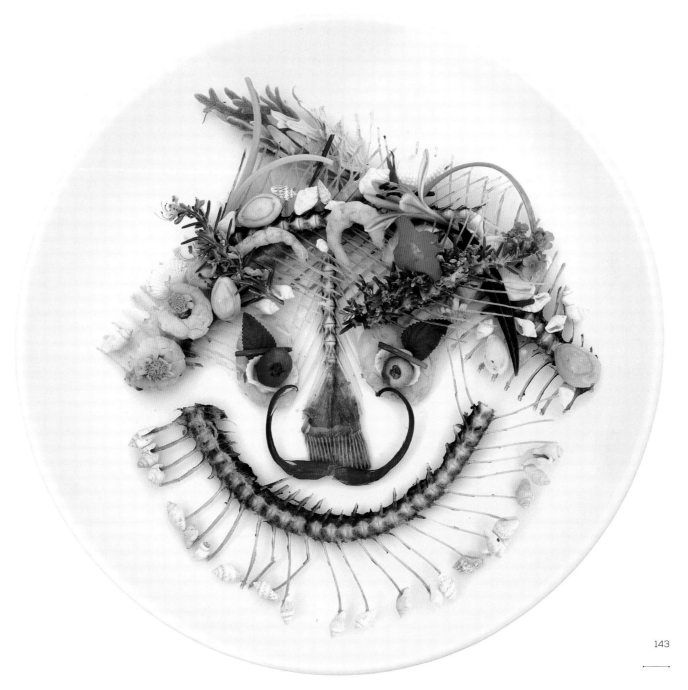

LEFTOVER SOLE

GRAINY
GRINS

PICK-ME-UP!

THE SHIPMATE

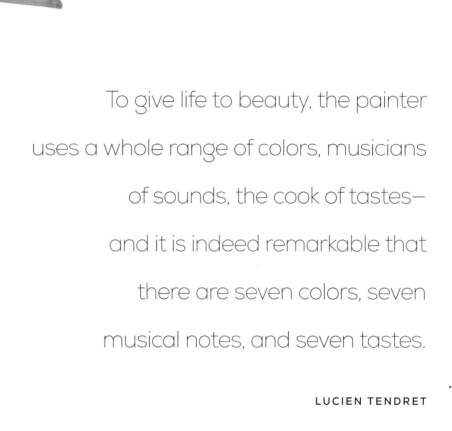

To give life to beauty, the painter

uses a whole range of colors, musicians

of sounds, the cook of tastes—

and it is indeed remarkable that

there are seven colors, seven

musical notes, and seven tastes.

HOMESPUN

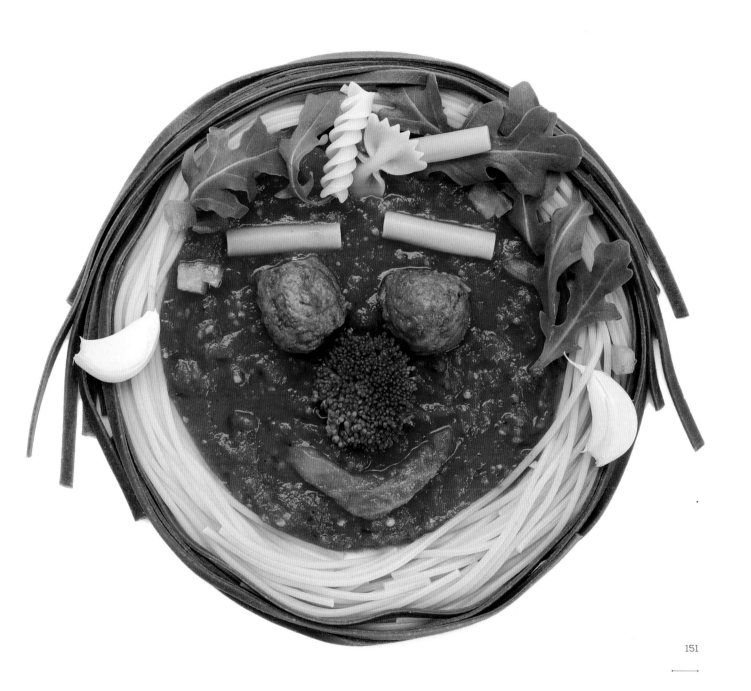

ROMA AMORE

DOCTOR HEAT

MY PAL BILL

Cooking is an art, but you eat it too.

MARCELLA HAZAN

WRAP ARTIST

KIM FU YA

FORBIDDEN LOTUS

ITALIAN KISS

CRANKY RISOTTO

Cookery is naturally the most
ancient of the arts, as of all arts
it is the most important.

GEORGE ELLWANGER

SPANISH LOVE

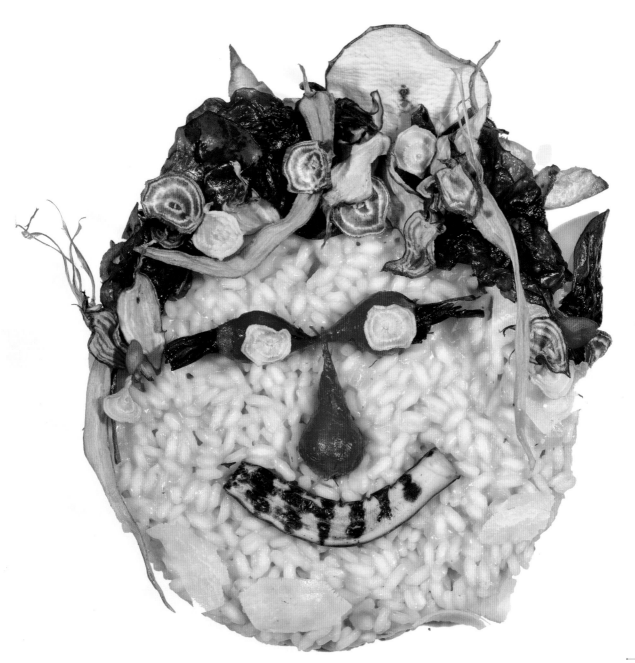

JUST MARCO

SWEET
SMILES

166

CHOCOLATE MISCHIEF

A DAY AT THE PEACH

I LOVE YOU!

KLIMT GLIMPSE

ESKIMO KISS

Spread love everywhere you go.

Let no one ever come to

you without leaving happier.

MOTHER THERESA

DUTCH SPRINKLES OF LOVE

MADEMOISELLE FROMAGE

CHRISTMAS TIMI

SWEETIE LIME PIE

DEEPLY CACAO

NUTTY LION

SMITHY MACAROONY

Gastronomy is the joy

of all conditions and all ages.

It adds wit to beauty.

CHARLES PIERRE MONSELET

MY SWEETHEART

ORANGE KISS

CHEF'S ESPRESSO

COOKIE LOVE

DARLING NANA

IVORY

TWISTED SISTER

BEDROOM EYES

THE FACE OF GRATITUDE

I believe that gratitude is the key that unlocks the door to every other blessing in life. Perhaps I've been so very blessed throughout my life because I have always been so truly thankful for the support, the loyalty, the interest, the generosity, the friendship, and the talent of my family, friends, and colleagues. It is my honor to thank all of those who provide optimism and fresh inspiration.

When I finish a book, it's always hard to know who to thank first. There are always so many doing so much by way of adding their expertise, and/or simply their enthusiasm for my projects. There are a few people who typically show up at the end of the acknowledgments of my books—not because their contributions are in any way insignificant; in fact, they are so essential.

This time, I decided to put them first. These are my word people. This is the least word-dense book I have created to date—most of my other works are culinary art cookbooks with far more text than photographs. So in *Food Faces*, when the work was thinner but the inspiration was as thick as ever, I bow to my two favorite wordsmiths: Marcelle Langan, my incredible writer, and Monica Velgos, my ever-diligent, eagle-eyed, and passionately meticulous copyeditor.

I send a special shout-out to Arnold Donald, President and Chief Executive Officer of Carnival Corporation & plc, whose leadership of these organizations is always an inspiration.

I'd specifically like to thank Stein Kruse, Chief Executive Officer and Group CEO of Holland America Group and Carnival UK; Orlando Ashford, President of Holland America; and Michael J. Smith, Senior Vice President of Guest Experience & Product Development for Holland America, for their unflagging support of my culinary vision. Thank you for the work you do and for your steadfast belief in my projects.

Thank you to Jan Swartz, Group President of Princess Cruises and Carnival Australia, who, whenever she saw any of my food faces, told me they made her cheerful and encouraged me not to give up on my belief in this project; Josh Leibowitz, Chief Strategy Officer of Carnival plc & Senior Vice President of Cunard Nord America, who came up with the name Face of Gratitude; as well as Roger Frizzel, Chief Communications Officer of Carnival plc, who extended his support.

Most importantly, thank you to the people who have worked with me directly on a daily basis and indirectly: John Mulvaney, Corporate Chef – Culinary Director; and Senior Executive Chefs, Robert Schuman, Jones Colin, Marco Marrama, and to those thousands of chefs and service-staff members, with whom I have had the pleasure to serve.

Thank you to project editor Tricia Levi and designer Susi Oberhelman, and to the entire Rizzoli and Welcome Books publishing team. And thank you to Franz Franc, whose original genius design ideas always inspire and keep me going.

THE FACE OF FAMILY

I dedicate this book to my family:

ANNEMARIE, my wonderful partner, who has a keen eye for refinement,
an appreciation of beauty, and an endless sense of wonder and optimism.

My own children:

MAGNUS, a professional artist himself, who advised me, "Food is an element of the
natural world, but to shape it, through figuration and abstraction, it becomes art";

KENNETH, who has a bachelor's degree in economics from
the University of Wisconsin and a master's degree in hospitality
management & real estate from FIU, and who provided critical feedback;

KRISTINA, who cherishes the work I do, and tells me so,
and who has emerged with her own brilliant light of creativity.

Welcome Books®
An imprint of Rizzoli International Publications, Inc.
300 Park Avenue South | New York, NY 10010 | www.rizzoliusa.com

Copyright © 2017 Rudi Sodamin
Designer: Susi Oberhelman

Library of Congress Catalog Control Number: 2017936158 | ISBN-13: 978-1-59962-142-5

2017 2018 2019 2020 / 10 9 8 7 6 5 4 3 2 1

Printed in China

PAGE 2: Theater of Mood Faces • PAGE 4: Señor Tortilla • PAGE 6: Rudi at work • PAGE 8: Chocolate Truffle Eyes
PAGE 10: Rudi Sodamin–Culinary Pop Artist • PAGE 13: Kristin 's Flatbread BFF • PAGES 14–15: G'day, mate! • PAGES 42–43: Mr. Aurora
PAGES 102–103: Crazy Chef Burger • PAGES 144–145: Lover's Lips • PAGES 164–165: My Indulgences • PAGE 191: Simple Love XO

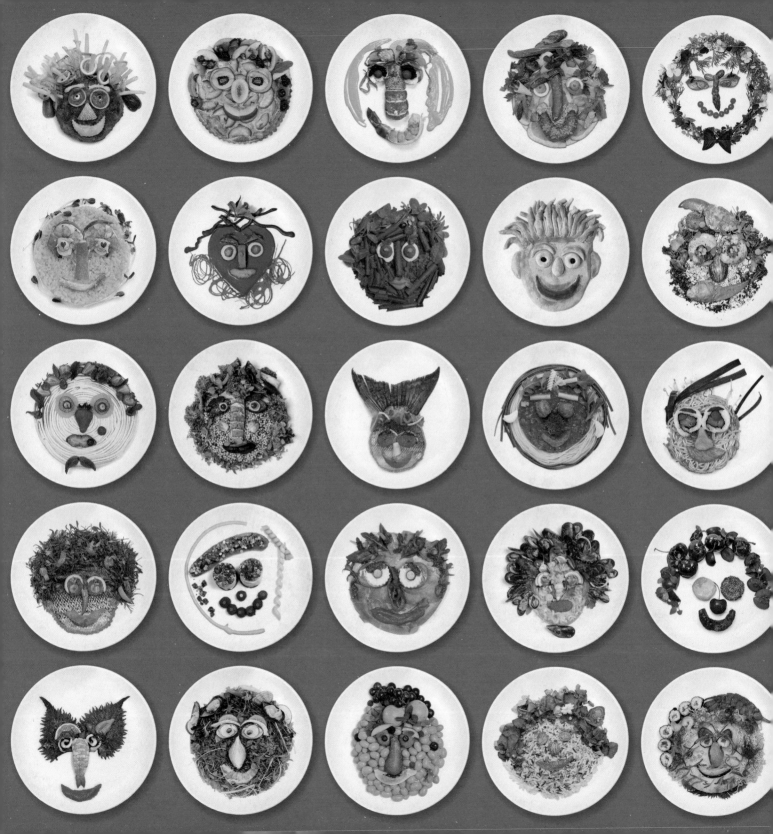